The Thanksgiving Parade

•The Good News Kids Learn about Faithfulness•

The Good News Kids Series

Worms for Winston: The Good News Kids Learn about Love
Fire Truck Friends: The Good News Kids Learn about Joy
Aqua Kid Saves the Day: The Good News Kids Learn about Peace
Springtime Special: The Good News Kids Learn about Patience
One Big Family: The Good News Kids Learn about Kindness
The Trouble with Trevor: The Good News Kids Learn about Goodness
The Thanksgiving Parade: The Good News Kids Learn about Faithfulness
The Big Secret: The Good News Kids Learn about Gentleness
God Is Everywhere: The Good News Kids Learn about Self-Control

Copyright © 1993 Concordia Publishing House
3558 S. Jefferson Avenue, St. Louis, MO 63118-3968
Manufactured in the United States of America

Library of Congress Cataloging-in-Publication Data

Mock, Dorothy K., 1941–
   The Thanksgiving Parade : the Good News Kids learn about faithfulness / Dorothy K. Mock : illustrated by
   Kathy Mitter.(Good News Kids Series)
   Summary: The Good New Kids find a way to participate in the Thanksgiving parade and to show they are
grateful for all God's blessings.
   ISBN 0-570-04743-9
   [1. Christian Life—Fiction. 2 Parades—Fiction.]I. Mitter, Kathy, ill. II. Title. III. Series: Mock, Dorothy K., 1941-
Good News Kids.
P27.M7129Th 1993
[E]—dc20   93-2988

---

1   2   3   4   5   6   7   8   9   10   02   01   00   99   98   97   96   95   94   93

The Thanksgiving Parade

•The Good News Kids Learn about Faithfulness•

Dorothy K. Mock

Illustrated by Kathy Mitter

Publishing House
St. Louis

It was a lazy, hazy, autumn afternoon. One of those not-much-to-do Saturdays that feels like it might last forever. The Good News Kids were playing a game of hopscotch when a truck loaded with lumber rumbled past. Mr. Milner, the apartment manager, was driving.

"Hey! Mr. Milner!" The kids shouted and waved.

Mr. Milner smiled and waved back.

The kids were excited. Sometimes on days like today (when there was nowhere to go and not much to play), Mr. Milner gave them jobs to do. They hurried along the path that led to Mr. Milner's parking place.

Mr. Milner was stacking the wood in his storage shed.

"What's all this wood for, Mr. Milner?" Winston asked. "Are you planning to make us a clubhouse or something?"

"We need a clubhouse," Brad said.

"We had a playhouse at my preschool," Amanda said dreamily. "It had little blue-and-white checkered curtains hanging in the window. And it had a little bell that you could ring on the front of the door." Amanda sighed. "I miss that playhouse," she said. "I really do."

"A clubhouse is different!" Harry hollered. "A clubhouse has a sign that reads 'NO GIRLS ALLOWED' on the front of the door. Not a bell!"

Mr. Milner pulled a picture from a pile of papers stacked on the front seat of his truck. "I *am* going to make a little house with this wood," he said. "A little apartment house. Your parents, and your friends and neighbors who live in these apartments, are going to help me."

He held the picture so the kids could see. "Ta-da!" he said. "Our float for the Thanksgiving parade."

Trevor bent forward to get a better look. "That's *my* house!" he shouted.

"Silly! We all live in an apartment like that," Teresa said. "That's why everybody wants to help make this float. Isn't it, Mr. Milner?"

"The Bible says we should give thanks to God for everything in Jesus' name," Mr. Milner said. "Making this float is one way we can say, 'Thank You, God! Thank You for being so faithful in all Your promises to us.' "

"Faith-full?" asked Trevor. "What's that?"

"It means God does what He says He'll do," smiled Amanda.

"That's right," said Mr. Milner. "He promised to send His own Son Jesus as our Savior, and He kept that promise. He promises to take care of us. He is faithful to all His promises. Our float will say, 'Thank You, God, for the gift of a good home. Thank You for giving us the talent we need to make a float.' "

Then Mr. Milner nodded his head up and down. He spoke very softly. "It's also a way for us to tell others about our faith in God. We can let everybody know how good He is."

"Can we help?" Brad wanted to know.

"We'll see," said Mr. Milner. "Next Saturday, when we start to work on it."

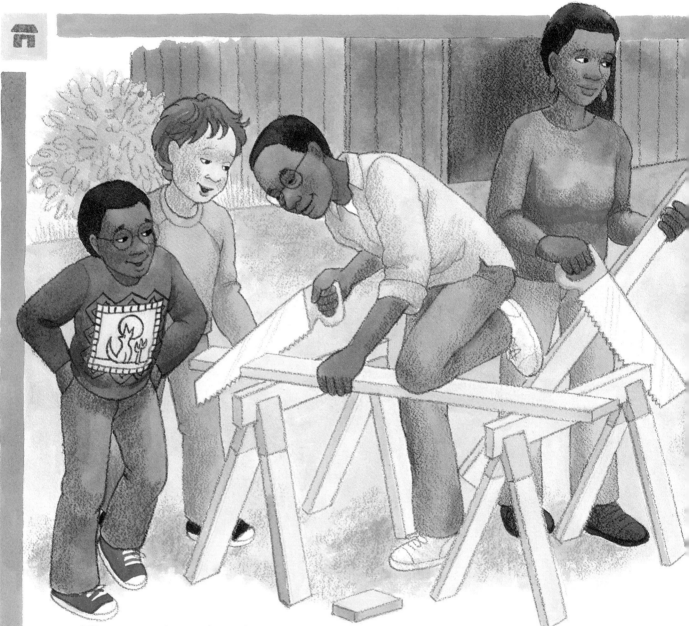

The next Saturday there was a lot of float-making work to be done. Some people were measuring and marking. Some people were sawing. Some people were hammering and nailing. Amanda's mom was measuring.

"May we help measure, Mom?" Amanda asked.

"Do you know how to measure?" her mom asked.

"No," Amanda said. "Is measuring a talent?"

"Maybe," Amanda's mom said. "It's something I know how to do. It's a way I can help."

Winston's parents were busy sawing wood.

"May we help saw that wood?" Winston asked.

"Do you know how to saw wood?" his dad asked.

"No," Winston said. "Is sawing your talent?"

"Maybe," his dad said. "It's something I know how to do. It's a way I can help."

Harry's dad and Mr. Milner were hammering and nailing.

"May we help?" Harry asked. "We want to help."

"Do you know how to make windows and a door and little wooden floors?" Harry's dad asked.

"No," Harry told his dad. "Is that your talent?"

"Of course it's my talent, Harry!" his dad almost shouted. "I'm a carpenter!" Then Harry's dad said, "It's something I know how to do. It's a way I can help."

Brad said, "Everybody is talented. There is measuring talent and sawing talent and hammering talent. Everybody else gets to say thank You to God with their talents. Why can't we be talented?"

"Don't worry," Mr. Milner said. "God gives everybody a talent—something they can do well, a way to thank God for His faithfulness. You'll find a way to say 'Thank You, God!' You'll find a job to do."

Ms. Meranda's Toe Tapping Teens had a job. They were going to march in front of the float and carry the apartment banner.

The kids watched Ms. Meranda in the laundry room. She was teaching the Teens a new dance for marching.

"Hop! Shuffle! Step! Hop! Shuffle! Step!" Ms. Meranda said.

Click! Clickety-click! Click! Clickety-click! went the Toe Tapping Teens.

The kids listened to what Ms. Meranda said. They watched Ms. Meranda when she showed the Teens what to do.

"Hop! Shuffle! Step! Hop! Shuffle! Step!" Teresa shouted. She wanted Ms. Meranda to know that they were practicing too.

"That dance is easy," Teresa told Ms. Meranda when her class was through. "May we march in the parade with you?"

"Oh, my, no," Ms. Meranda said. "Little legs weren't made for miles of marching."

The Apartment People Band had a job. They were going to play the tunes for the Toe Tapping Teens from the back of the truck that would pull the float. The Apartment People Band was practicing outside. Drums were booming. Trumpets were tooting.

The Good News Kids stood close to the leader of the band. They swayed this way and that way to the music. They clapped their hands. They tapped their feet.

"We want to be in the parade too," Winston told the band leader when the band stopped. "May we ride in the back of the truck? We can hold your music for you."

The band leader laughed. "It will take a miracle to squeeze the trumpets, trombones, and a tuba in the back of that truck!" he said. "There is no room for boys and girls to hold our music."

The next day the Good News Kids were still sad as they sat around the sandbox smoothing the sand to clear a landing strip for their space shuttle. They were tired of worrying about talents. They were tired of looking for something to do.

Trevor was humming. The tune was "Jesus Loves Me." It was a song all the kids knew.

Winston was thinking. He was thinking about parades and Thanksgiving. He was thinking about talents. He was humming "Jesus Loves Me" too.

Suddenly Winston had an idea. He said, "I know something we can do! I know a way that we can help!" And he told the kids all about it.

Harry hollered, "All right! Tomorrow we can tell Mr. Milner!"

"It's a great idea," Mr. Milner said with a smile. "You'll have to practice. But it's something that you know how to do. It's a way that you can help."

THE APARTMENT HOUSE FLOAT

It was a wonderful parade. All the floats were decorated to show what people were thankful for. There was a fish float, a fruit float, and a vegetable float. There was a Sunday school float and a church float.

The floats lined up one after the other along the street.
First came Ms. Meranda and the Toe Tapping Teens. Then came the Apartment People Band and the Apartment House float.
Boom-ditty! Boom-ditty! Boom! Boom! Boom! went the band.
Click! Clickety-click! Click! Clickety-click! went the Toe Tapping Teens.

Suddenly the music stopped. The little apartment house door opened. Out came the Good News Kids! They stood on the float and started to sing. They sang words that Winston had made up to the tune of "Jesus Loves Me."

Thanks to God for everything;
Thanks to God in Jesus' name.
This song is one way we say,
"Thank You, God, for this fine day!"

All along the street people clapped and cheered.

"I knew you could do it," Mr. Milner said after the parade. "I knew I could count on you to help."

"It was fun!" Winston said.

"But it was work!" Harry hollered. "We had to find a talent. Then we had to practice the talent. And we had to share our talent to tell everybody about God."

Brad staggered around like he was going to fall. He said, "I get tired just thinking about it."

"It *is* work to be faithful about finishing a job, or even to be faithful about doing what God wants us to do," Mr. Milner said. "But it's work that God helps us do. He is always faithful to us. He never gives up on us. And He sent Jesus to show us how to love Him and be faithful to Him. Even when we feel sad, or don't know what to do, God keeps us close."

"Does God pay helpers?" Trevor wanted to know.

"God pays His helpers with happy feelings," Teresa said.

"Sometimes God pays His helpers with little houses," said Mr. Milner. He waved his arm toward the Apartment House float.

The kids' eyes grew big and round. Their mouths dropped open. They stared at Mr. Milner.

"That's right," he said. "The house is yours. You told me you needed one for a clubhouse."

The kids were very quiet. Something was swelling deep inside them. Something like thankfulness or faithfulness or love. The kids couldn't think of a thing to say. Even Harry couldn't think of a thing to say. So the Good News Kids crowded around Mr. Milner and started to sing:

Thanks to God for everything;
Thanks to God in Jesus' name.
This song is one way we say,
"Thank You, God, for this fine day!"